BEGINNING TO END

Cotton to T-shirt

by Rachel Grack

BLASTOFF! READERS 2

BELLWETHER MEDIA • MINNEAPOLIS, MN

Note to Librarians, Teachers, and Parents:

Blastoff! Readers are carefully developed by literacy experts and combine standards-based content with developmentally appropriate text.

Level 1 provides the most support through repetition of high-frequency words, light text, predictable sentence patterns, and strong visual support.

Level 2 offers early readers a bit more challenge through varied simple sentences, increased text load, and less repetition of high-frequency words.

Level 3 advances early-fluent readers toward fluency through increased text and concept load, less reliance on visuals, longer sentences, and more literary language.

Level 4 builds reading stamina by providing more text per page, increased use of punctuation, greater variation in sentence patterns, and increasingly challenging vocabulary.

Level 5 encourages children to move from "learning to read" to "reading to learn" by providing even more text, varied writing styles, and less familiar topics.

Whichever book is right for your reader, Blastoff! Readers are the perfect books to build confidence and encourage a love of reading that will last a lifetime!

This edition first published in 2020 by Bellwether Media, Inc.

No part of this publication may be reproduced in whole or in part without written permission of the publisher. For information regarding permission, write to Bellwether Media, Inc., Attention: Permissions Department, 6012 Blue Circle Drive, Minnetonka, MN 55343.

Library of Congress Cataloging-in-Publication Data

Names: Koestler-Grack, Rachel A., 1973- author.
Title: Cotton to T-shirt / Rachel Grack.
Description: Minneapolis : Bellwether Media, 2020. | Series: Beginning to end |
  Includes bibliographical references and index. | Audience: Ages 5-8 | Audience: Grades K-1 |
  Summary: "Relevant images matchinformative text in this introduction to how t-shirts are made.
  Intended for students in kindergarten through third grade"– Provided by publisher.
Identifiers: LCCN 2019026687 (print) | LCCN 2019026688 (ebook) |
  ISBN 9781644871393 (library binding) | ISBN 9781618918093 (ebook)
Subjects: LCSH: Textile industry–Juvenile literature. | T-shirts–Juvenile literature.
Classification: LCC HD9889.Y29 K64 2020 (print) | LCC HD9889.Y29 (ebook) | DDC 687/.115–dc23
LC record available at https://lccn.loc.gov/2019026687
LC ebook record available at https://lccn.loc.gov/2019026688

Editor: Rebecca Sabelko   Designer: Laura Sowers

Printed in the United States of America, North Mankato, MN.

Table of Contents

T-shirt Beginnings

How was your favorite T-shirt made? It started in a field of cotton plants.

Where Does Cotton Grow?

India produces 6.8 million tons (6.2 million metric tons) of cotton each year.

White, fluffy cotton **bolls** became the clothes you wear!

Field to Fabric

cotton picker

The cotton is ready to **harvest**! Farmers drive **cotton pickers** through the fields.

Pickers gather seed cotton into huge **bales**. The cotton is ready for the **gin**!

seed cotton bales

Gins dry and clean the cotton. They also remove seeds from the cotton **fibers**.

Cleaned fibers get pressed into bales.

cleaned fiber bales

gin

T-shirt Water Usage

713 gallons
(2,700 liters)
of water needed
to make one T-shirt

carding machine

Fibers from the bales are **carded** and **combed** into thin webs.

10

Machines pull the webs into thick strands to create **slivers**.

cotton sliver
↓

The **roving process** prepares the fibers for spinning.

Roving pulls the sliver to a size that can be spun. Then the sliver is wrapped onto **bobbins**.

bobbins

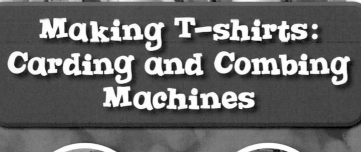

Making T-shirts: Carding and Combing Machines

carding machine

combing machine

roving machine

It is time to spin the yarn!
Spinning machines pull and
twist the yarn to add strength.

spinning machine

This creates a good yarn for cloth.

cotton fabric

Machines turn the yarn into **fabric**. T-shirts are made of **knit** cotton. This cloth is soft, stretchy, and breathable. It makes comfy clothes!

Cotton to T-shirt

1

harvest cotton and put
cotton through gin

2

card the cotton

3

rove and spin the
cotton into yarn

4

turn yarn into fabric

5

sew into a T-shirt!

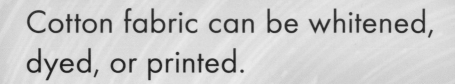

Cotton fabric can be whitened, dyed, or printed.

Then it is finished!
Clothing companies sew
the fabric into T-shirts.

T-shirts!

Your T-shirt can be any color. Maybe there is a picture printed on it.

T-shirts have many looks.
But they all began
as cotton bolls!

Glossary

bales—large bundles of cotton that are tied tightly together

bobbins—cylinder-shaped objects that hold yarn or thread

bolls—round, fluffy balls on a cotton plant

carded—cleaned and straightened

combed—straightened to make longer, stronger fibers

cotton pickers—farm machines that pick cotton bolls from the plants

fabric—a type of cloth

fibers—thread

gin—a machine that separates cotton from its seed

harvest—to gather crops

knit—related to cloth made by looping yarn together

roving process—a system that lightly twists fibers

slivers—soft, thick strands of cotton

To Learn More

AT THE LIBRARY

Butterworth, Chris. *Where Did My Clothes Come From?* Sommerville, Mass.: Candlewick Press, 2015.

Hayes, Amy. *Turning Wool into Sweaters*. New York, N.Y.: Cavendish Square Publishing, 2016.

Meister, Cari. *From Cotton to T-shirts*. Mankato, Minn.: Amicus Illustrated, 2020.

ON THE WEB

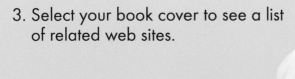

FACTSURFER

Factsurfer.com gives you a safe, fun way to find more information.

1. Go to www.factsurfer.com.

2. Enter "cotton to T-shirt" into the search box and click 🔍.

3. Select your book cover to see a list of related web sites.

Index

The images in this book are reproduced through the courtesy of: xiaorui, front cover (shirts); robdimagery, front cover (cotton); Valentina Razumova, p. 3; Phillip Minnis, pp. 4-5; AJ Laing, pp. 6-7, 17 (1); Mark Winfrey, p. 7; YusufAslan, p. 8; Paul R. Jones, pp. 8-9; gyn9037, pp. 10, 13 (left), 15, 17 (2); zhengzaishuru, pp. 10-11; Marbury, p. 12; Arterra/ Getty Images, pp. 12-13; Wikimedia Commons, p. 13 (right); Joerg Boethling/ Alamy, pp. 14-15, 18-19; danishkhan, p. 16; Alba_alioth, p. 17 (3); moxumbic, p. 17 (4); michaeljung, p. 17 (5); AdaCo, p. 19; Africa Studio, pp. 20-21; Asia Images Group, p. 21; iamtui7, p. 23.